What's in this book

This book belongs to

_____

T0351535

郑和下西洋 Zheng He's voyages

学习内容 Contents

沟通 Communication

说说旅行经历
Talk about travel experiences

说说服装
Talk about clothes

背景介绍：
郑和，中国明代的航海家，带领着庞大的船队从中国出发远航到其他国家。

生词 New words

⭐ 从	from
⭐ 到	to
⭐ 旅行	to travel
⭐ 国家	country
⭐ 出发	to set out
⭐ 短裤	shorts
⭐ 大衣	coat
⭐ 毛衣	sweater, jumper
年轻	young
事情	affair
漂亮	beautiful
衬衫	shirt

句式 Sentence patterns

从1405年到1433年，他进行了七次航海旅行。

He had seven sea voyages from 1405 to 1433.

从中国到美国，我可以坐飞机。

I can travel by air from China to America.

跨学科学习 Project

调查上海天气并设计旅行计划

Research the weather in Shanghai and plan a trip

文化 Cultures

中西方城市的标志性建筑

Landmarks of cities in the East and the West

参考答案：

1 Yes, I like travelling because I see more of the world./ No, travelling is not as fun as doing sports.

2 I have only taken a small boat trip on a river./ Yes I travelled from the UK to France by ship.

3 No, I don't know him./Yes, he is a famous Chinese navigator.

Get ready

1 Do you like travelling? Why?

2 Have you travelled by ship before?

3 Do you know the man in the picture?

故事大意：
简单介绍郑和下西洋的事迹，由此引出与学生实际生活相关的旅行话题。倡导行前准备对旅程的重要性。

生活中的一切活动和现象我们叫"事情"。

shì qing
事情

nián qīng
年轻

参考问题和答案：

1 Do you know this young man? (Yes, he is Zheng He, a great Chinese navigator./No.)

2 Do you know why he is well known? (Yes, he led a fleet and sailed from China to many other countries./No.)

郑和下西洋，或称"珍宝航行"，是泛中国明代早期 1405 年至 1433 年间的场连续的大规模远洋航海，跨越了东地区、印度次大陆、阿拉伯半岛、及非各地，被认为是当时世界上规模最的远洋航海项目。

你认识这个年轻人吗？你知道中国古代郑和航海的事情吗？

4

从1405年到1433年，明成祖命郑和率领庞大船队远航。郑和船队七次下西洋的总航程达到七万多海里，长度相当于地球圆周的三倍多。

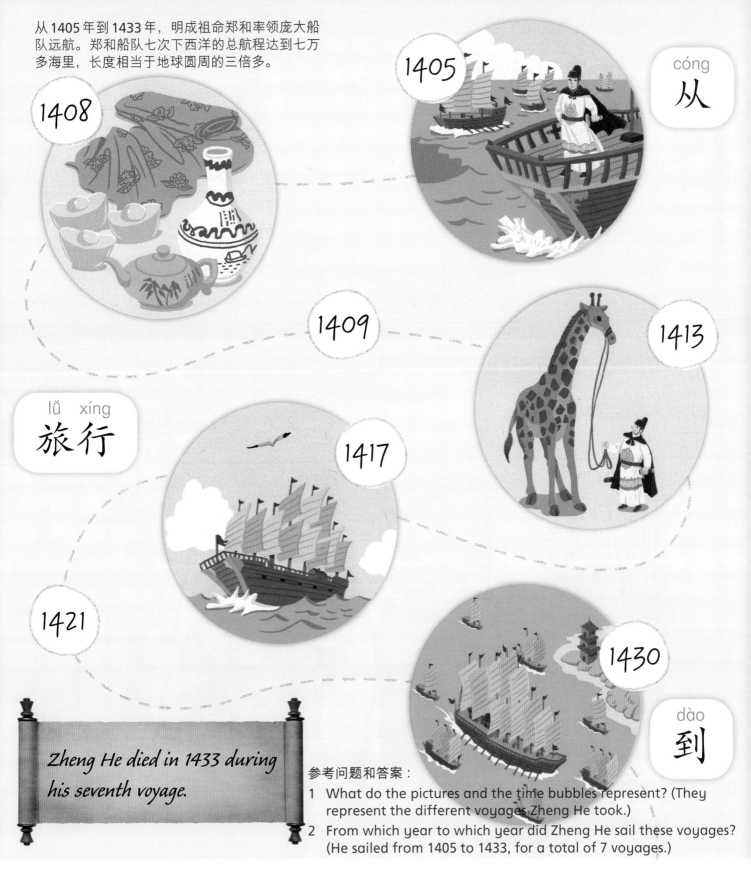

1408

1405

cóng
从

1409

1413

lǚ xíng
旅行

1417

1421

1430

dào
到

Zheng He died in 1433 during his seventh voyage.

参考问题和答案：

1 What do the pictures and the time bubbles represent? (They represent the different voyages Zheng He took.)

2 From which year to which year did Zheng He sail these voyages? (He sailed from 1405 to 1433, for a total of 7 voyages.)

从1405年到1433年，郑和用二十八年的时间，进行了七次航海旅行。

郑和率领二百四十多只海船和二万七千四百名航员拜访了三十余个西太平洋和印度洋的国家和地区。

guó jiā
国家

他带领二百四十多只船，去了三十多个国家和地区。

参考问题和答案：

1　Can you guess how many ships there are in the fleet?
(There are over twenty/a hundred ships.)

2　Which country do you think the fleet is arriving at?
(I think it is India./I am not sure.)

chū fā

出发

参考问题和答案：

1 Is the girl with the telescope ready to set out?
(Yes, she has packed her luggage and is ready
to go.)

2 Do you like to travel on land or on sea more?
(I like to travel on land more because I get sea
sick when I take the ship./I like both.)

你想像郑和一样，从你的国家出发，
探索大陆和大海吗？

pìào liang
漂亮

从这个国家到那个国家，我们可以看漂亮的风景。

参考问题和答案：

1 Do you like the scenery in the pictures? (Yes, it looks beautiful./I don't like the snow. It is not pretty.)

2 Are the statues and the buildings beautiful? (Yes, they are.)

dà yī
大衣

máo yī
毛衣

chèn shān
衬衫

duǎn kù
短裤

参考问题和答案：

1 Are the girls on the top right hand side of the page properly dressed for the weather? (No, one of them doesn't have an umbrella and the other is not dressed warm enough.)

2 Do you think we should properly prepare before travelling? (Yes, so that the travelling can be more fun.)

去旅行，应该穿短裤还是大衣？衬衫还是毛衣？做好准备会更完美。

Let's think

1 Recall the story. Circle the correct answers.

1 Where did Zheng He start each voyage?

   (a) 中国   b 英国   c 美国

2 When did Zheng He start his first voyage?

   a 1433   b 1408   (c) 1405

3 How many countries and regions did Zheng He go to?

   a 十多个   b 二十多个   (c) 三十多个

2 Discuss your favourite way to travel with your friend. You may draw your own idea. 参考表达见下方。

你喜欢怎么去旅行？

我喜欢坐船去旅行，因为我最喜欢大海。
我觉得夏天坐船最好。

我喜欢坐……去
旅行。因为……

我喜欢坐火车去旅行，因为火车很
舒服，我也喜欢看窗外面的风景。

我喜欢坐飞机去旅行，因为
我喜欢从天上看地上的城市。

New words

延伸活动：

学生三人一组根据本图生词编小故事，并向全班演讲，看看哪组的故事说得最好最有趣。如：我们来说说这件事情——妈妈和玲玲要去旅行，出发前，她们去买衣服。这里有毛衣、大衣、衬衫和短裤，它们都很漂亮。我想她们要从美国到中国去，她们买的衬衫可能是给朋友的礼物。

02

1 Learn the new words.

2 Listen to your teacher and point to the correct words above.

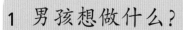

03 **1** Listen and circle the correct answers.

04 **2** Look at the pictures. Listen to the story ar

1 男孩想做什么？

　　a 跳舞

　　b 唱歌

　　ⓒ 旅行

你们喜欢旅行吗？

喜欢！从去年到今年，我们已经去了三个国家。

2 男孩从哪个国家出发？

　　a 英国

　　ⓑ 美国

　　c 中国

3 男孩不会带什么衣服？

　　a 大衣

　　b 毛衣

　　ⓒ 短裤

男孩是冬天去英国，那里很冷，他说会带大衣和毛衣去，因此我们可以假设他不会带短裤去。

下雨了，我们去那边。

雨真大！

第一题录音稿：

女孩：你圣诞节想做什么？
男孩：我想和爸爸妈妈去旅行，从美国出发到英国。
女孩：你们坐飞机去吗？
男孩：是。英国的冬天很冷，但是很漂亮。
女孩：多穿点衣服，别感冒了。
男孩：好。我会带几件大衣和毛衣去英国。

我最喜欢夏天去有海的国家。

我也喜欢！可以穿漂亮的衬衫和短裤。

妈妈，你怎么知道会下雨？

因为我做好了准备。

3 Look at the photos and talk to your friend.

他们从哪里出发？

北京

他们从……北京……出发。

从家里到操场，她们怎么去？

她们从家里走路去操场。

她穿了什么衣服？

她穿了毛衣、长裤和大衣。

第二题参考问题和答案：

1 What kind of countries do Hao Hao and Elsa like to travel to? (They like to go to countries by the sea.)

2 What kind of countries do you like to travel to? (I like to travel to countries with interesting zoos/good food/beautiful scenery.)

13

Task

鼓励学生在听了同学的分享后，可向同学发问，通过交流提高中文表达能力。

Paste a photo of your favourite trip. Talk about it with your friend.

去年，我们从美国出发，去英国旅行。英国的城市很漂亮。

今年冬天，我和爸爸、妈妈一起去旅行。那里下雪了，很冷，但是很好玩。

Paste your photo here.

……年，我从……到……我最喜欢……

Game

Play with your friend. Pick a card and say the word aloud. Ask your friend to say the opposite.

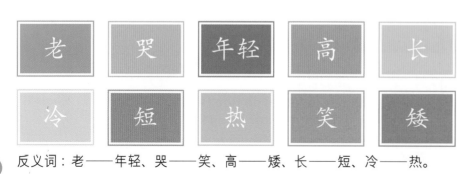

| 老 | 哭 | 年轻 | 高 | 长 |
| 冷 | 短 | 热 | 笑 | 矮 |

哭

反义词：老——年轻、哭——笑、高——矮、长——短、冷——热。

Chant

🎧 05 **Listen and say.**

学生可分两组，一组说唱的时候，另一组听歌词并用手指向对应的图画。然后对调角色。

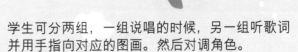

英国、美国和中国，
旅行记得加上我。
要做的事情不多，
我们可以一起做。
大衣、毛衣和衬衫，
短裤、长裤和袜子，
大家一起准备好。
出发旅行带背包，
开心一笑拍拍照。

生活用语 Daily expressions

够了吗？
Is that enough?

让我来。
Let me do it.

15

写一写 Write

1 Trace and write the characters.

丿 从 从 从

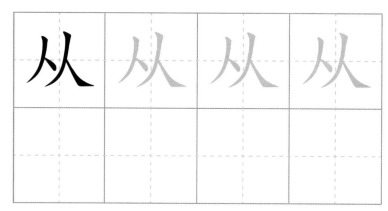

提醒学生"从"字的左右两个部件不相同，笔画顺序为"撇、点、撇、捺"。

乚 乚 出 出 出
一 ㇒ 发 发 发

2 Write and say.

<u>从</u> 去年到今年，我去了很多地方。

我们一起<u>出发</u>去旅行了。

3 Fill in the blanks with the correct words. Colour the clothes using the same colours.

| 从 | 出发 | 衣 | 雨 |
| 绿色 | 蓝色 | 黄色 | 粉色 |

今天 <u>出发</u> 前，妈妈说："你看看窗外的天气，可能会下<u>雨</u>。"我穿上毛<u>衣</u>和雨<u>衣</u>，准备了<u>雨</u>伞。<u>从</u>家里<u>出发</u>后，已经开始下<u>雨</u>了。

拼音输入法 Pinyin input

Write the Pinyin above the words with the leaves and type the paragraph. Check with your friends to see who can finish first.

今年秋天（qiū tiān），我们坐船（chuán）去中国旅行（lǚ xíng）。

我最喜欢秋天（qiū tiān），因为风景很漂亮。我可以穿我喜欢的大衣（dà yī）和毛衣（máo yī）。我们学了功夫（gōngfu），看见了熊猫，还知道了很多中国的事情。

延伸活动：
做完题目后，学生两人一组互相朗读段落一次。

Cultures

延伸活动：
认识了下面的四个标志性建筑后，学生可上网继续探索世界上其他国家或地区的一些有名建筑，并与全班分享有关资讯。

Every big city has something interesting to see. Learn about the landmarks below. Which one would you like to visit? Tell your friend about it.

从美国到中国，我们可以坐飞机。我想去北京旅行，去看看……

Beijing, China

紫禁城，现称北京故宫，是明清两个朝代二十四位皇帝的皇宫，现存规模最大的宫殿型建筑。它位于北京中轴线的中心，于1420年落成。

The Forbidden City, located in the centre of Beijing, was home to the 24 emperors of the Ming and the Qing dynasties.

Agra, India

泰姬陵是一座用白色大理石建造的陵墓，是莫卧儿王朝第5代皇帝沙贾汗为了纪念他的第二任妻子而兴建的，位于印度北方邦阿格拉，于1654年落成。

The Taj Mahal, a marble building, was commissioned by a Mughal emperor in memory of his wife.

它真漂亮，你想去吗？

它非常高。很多人知道它。你喜欢这个国家吗？

Paris, France

艾菲尔铁塔是位于法国巴黎战神广场的铁制镂空塔，世界著名建筑，也是法国文化象征之一。它于1889年落成。

The Eiffel Tower, an iron tower named after its engineer Gustave Eiffel, is 324 metres tall. It is the icon of France.

自由女神像是自由和美国的象征。它位于美国纽约曼哈顿纽约港，是法国送给美国的礼物，于1886年落成。塑像女性身穿长袍，代表罗马神话中的自主神。

The Statue of Liberty, a sculpture of the female figure Libertas, is the icon of freedom and of the United States.

New York, United States

这个城市真大！

Project

1 Talk about a holiday you had and show a photo to your friend.

> ……年，我去……旅行了。那里很漂亮，天气非常好。我穿衬衫和……去。从我的城市到那里，坐……最舒服。去旅行是我最喜欢的事情。

Paste your photo here.

2 Plan a trip to Shanghai during your favourite season. Research the weather and complete the table below. You may use some words more than once. Then tell your friend about your plan.

a 毛衣　b 短裤　c 大衣　d 衬衫　e 围巾

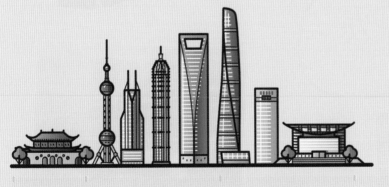

> 我想……去上海旅行，因为天气很……我……月从……出发。我会穿……和……我可以玩……

季节	春天	夏天	秋天	冬天
天气	5–18℃	21–28 ℃	9–17 ℃	4–12 ℃
衣服	a, b, d	b, d	a, d, e	a, c, d, e

温习 Checkpoint

延伸活动：
学生两人一组，一个说出日期，另一个朗读该日的日记内容，待朗读完所有内容后，互换角色，再重复一次。

1 Help the boy complete his holiday journal. Read what he says and write the characters.

8月3日

我最喜欢的事情是骑自行车。上午，我骑自行车去看电影。

8月1日

我

今天不太热，我和朋友一起去学校打篮球。

8月7日

我的阿姨很年轻，也很快乐。

我买了大衣和毛衣，还买了漂亮的……和……

8月12日

我们 从 家里 出 发 ，一起去中国旅行。

8月17日

8月22日

中国是我最想去的国家。从北京到上海，我们去了很多地方。

评核方法：

学生两人一组，互相考察评价表内单词和句子的听说读写。交际沟通部分由老师朗读要求，学生再互相对话。如果达到了某项技能要求，则用色笔将星星或小辣椒涂色。

2 Work with your friend. Colour the stars and the chillies.

Words	说	读	写
从	☆	☆	☆
到	☆	☆	🌶
旅行	☆	☆	🌶
国家	☆	☆	🌶
出发	☆	☆	☆
短裤	☆	☆	🌶
大衣	☆	☆	🌶
毛衣	☆	☆	🌶
年轻	☆	🌶	🌶
事情	☆	🌶	🌶

Words and sentences	说	读	写
漂亮	☆	🌶	🌶
衬衫	☆	🌶	🌶
从 1405 年到 1433 年，他进行了七次航海旅行。	☆	🌶	🌶
从中国到美国，我可以坐飞机。	☆	🌶	🌶

Talk about travel experiences	☆
Talk about clothes	☆

3 What does your teacher say?

评核建议：

根据学生课堂表现，分别给予"太棒了！(Excellent!)"、"不错！(Good!)"或"继续努力！(Work harder!)"的评价，再让学生圈出左侧对应的表情，以记录自己的学习情况。

My teacher says ...

21

分享 Sharing

延伸活动：
1 学生用手遮盖英文，读中文单词，并思考单词意思；
2 学生用手遮盖中文单词，看着英文说出对应的中文单词；
3 学生四人一组，尽量运用中文单词分角色复述故事。

Words I remember

从	cóng	from
到	dào	to
旅行	lǚ xíng	to travel
国家	guó jiā	country
出发	chū fā	to set out
短裤	duǎn kù	shorts
大衣	dà yī	coat
毛衣	máo yī	sweater, jumper
年轻	nián qīng	young
事情	shì qing	affair
漂亮	piào liang	beautiful
衬衫	chèn shān	shirt

Other words

郑和	zhèng hé	Zheng He
西洋	xī yáng	Western Seas
认识	rèn shi	to know
古代	gǔ dài	ancient times
航海	háng hǎi	navigation
进行	jìn xíng	to proceed
次	cì	time
带领	dài lǐng	to lead
地区	dì qū	area
探索	tàn suǒ	to explore
大陆	dà lù	continent
风景	fēng jǐng	scenery
应该	yīng gāi	should
准备	zhǔn bèi	to prepare
更	gèng	even more
完美	wán měi	perfect

OXFORD
UNIVERSITY PRESS

Oxford University Press is a department of the University of Oxford.
It furthers the University's objective of excellence in research, scholarship,
and education by publishing worldwide. Oxford is a registered trade mark of
Oxford University Press in the UK and in certain other countries

Published in Hong Kong by
Oxford University Press (China) Limited
39th Floor, One Kowloon, 1 Wang Yuen Street, Kowloon Bay,
Hong Kong

© Oxford University Press (China) Limited 2017

Illustrated by Ah Lun, Anne Lee, Emily Chan, KY Chan and Wildman

Photographs for reproduction permitted by Dreamstime.com

China National Publications Import & Export (Group) Corporation is an authorized distributor of
Oxford Elementary Chinese.

Please contact content@cnpiec.com.cn or 86-10-65856782

ISBN: 978-0-19-047009-8

10 9 8 7 6 5 4 3 2

Teacher's Edition
ISBN: 978-0-19-082317-7

10 9 8 7 6 5 4 3 2